SOUTH DAKOTA

The Mount Rushmore State

BY
JOHN HAMILTON

Abdo & Daughters

An imprint of Abdo Publishing | abdopublishing.com

abdopublishing.com

Published by ABDO Publishing, a division of ABDO, PO Box 398166, Minneapolis, Minnesota 55439. Copyright © 2017 by Abdo Consulting Group, Inc. International copyrights reserved in all countries. No part of this book may be reproduced in any form without written permission from the publisher. ABDO & Daughters™ is a trademark and logo of ABDO Publishing.

Printed in the United States of America, North Mankato, Minnesota.
072016
092016

THIS BOOK CONTAINS
RECYCLED MATERIALS

Editor: Sue Hamilton   **Contributing Editor:** Bridget O'Brien
Graphic Design: Sue Hamilton
Cover Art Direction: Candice Keimig   **Cover Photo Selection:** Neil Klinepier
Cover Photo: iStock
Interior Images: Aberdeen Area Convention and Visitors Bureau, Alamy, AP, Dreamstime, George Catlin, Getty, Granger, History in Full Color-Restoration/Colorization, Independence National Historical Park/C.W. Peale, iStock, John Hamilton, Karl Bodmer, Lawrence Berkeley National Laboratory, Library of Congress, Minden Pictures, Mile High Maps, Mountain High Maps, New York Public Library, One Mile Up, Sioux Falls Skyforce, South Dakota State University-Brookings, U.S. Air Force, U.S. Department of Agriculture, University of Nebraska State Museum, University of South Dakota-Vermillion, White House, and Wikimedia.

Statistics: *State and City Populations*, U.S. Census Bureau, July 1, 2015 estimates; *Land and Water Area*, U.S. Census Bureau, 2010 Census, MAF/TIGER database; *State Temperature Extremes*, NOAA National Climatic Data Center; *Climatology and Average Annual Precipitation*, NOAA National Climatic Data Center, 1980-2015 statewide averages; *State Highest and Lowest Points*, NOAA National Geodetic Survey.

Websites: To learn more about the United States, visit booklinks.abdopublishing.com. These links are routinely monitored and updated to provide the most current information available.

Cataloging-in-Publication Data

Names: Hamilton, John, 1959- author.
Title: South Dakota / by John Hamilton.
Description: Minneapolis, MN : Abdo Publishing, [2017] | Series: The United
    States of America | Includes index.
Identifiers: LCCN 2015957730 | ISBN 9781680783445 (lib. bdg.) |
    ISBN 9781680774481 (ebook)
Subjects: LCSH: South Dakota--Juvenile literature.
Classification: DDC 978.3--dc23
LC record available at http://lccn.loc.gov/2015957730

CONTENTS

THE
MOUNT RUSHMORE
STATE

What makes South Dakota unique? There are treeless, wide-open spaces, with rolling prairies, fertile farmland, and sprawling cattle ranches. There are forested mountains, with rocky spires that reach toward the blue Western sky. There are small farm towns, large Indian reservations, and bustling cities. There are lakes and mighty rivers, along with the bone-dry Badlands, with their steep ravines and rainbow-colored cliffs. Gold mines, Old West shoot-outs, a palace made of corn, herds of bison, zoos, dinosaurs, rodeos… the list goes on and on.

Most notable of all is Mount Rushmore National Memorial, a must-see sculpture carved into the side of a Black Hills mountain. More than 3 million people come each year to gaze up at the 60-foot (18-m) -high granite faces of Presidents George Washington, Thomas Jefferson, Theodore Roosevelt, and Abraham Lincoln. That is why South Dakota is nicknamed "The Mount Rushmore State."

A hiker looks across Badlands National Park. Paths wind through the rugged, fossil-filled rock formations.

Mount Rushmore National Monument was created by sculptor Gutzon Borglum. About 90 percent of the carving was done using dynamite. Jackhammers and hand chisels were used for the fine details. More than 400 carvers, many suspended by ropes, worked for 14 years until the monument was completed on October 31, 1941.

QUICK FACTS

Name: The word "Dakota" means "friend" or "ally" in the language of the Native American Sioux nation.

State Capital: Pierre, population 14,002

Date of Statehood: November 2, 1889 (40th state)

Population: 858,469 (46th-most populous state)

Area (Total Land and Water): 77,116 square miles (199,730 sq km), 17th-largest state

Largest City: Sioux Falls, population 171,544

Nickname: The Mount Rushmore State;
The Coyote State

Motto: Under God the People Rule

State Bird: Ring-Necked Pheasant

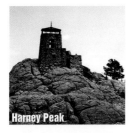

State Flower: Pasque

State Mineral: Rose Quartz

State Tree: Black Hills Spruce

State Song: "Hail, South Dakota"

Highest Point: Harney Peak, 7,242 feet (2,207 m)

Lowest Point: Big Stone Lake, 966 feet (294 m)

Average July High Temperature: 86°F (30°C)

Record High Temperature: 120°F (49°C), in Usta on July 15, 2006

Average January Low Temperature: 8°F (-13°C)

Record Low Temperature: -58°F (-50°C), in McIntosh on February 17, 1936

Average Annual Precipitation: 20 inches (51 cm)

Number of U.S. Senators: 2

Number of U.S. Representatives: 1

U.S. Postal Service Abbreviation: SD

GEOGRAPHY

South Dakota is in the Midwest region of the United States. It is also part of the Great Plains. It is a big state, covering 77,116 square miles (199,730 sq km). Minnesota and Iowa share its eastern border. To the south is Nebraska. To the west are Wyoming and Montana. North Dakota is to the north.

Thousands of years ago, huge sheets of ice called glaciers scraped and formed the land under the eastern half of South Dakota. They stopped about where the Missouri River is today. The river runs north and south, nearly splitting the state up the middle.

The Missouri River approaches Pierre, South Dakota. The river runs north and south through the state, nearly splitting it up the middle.

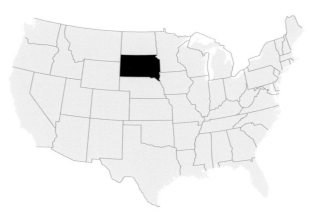

South Dakota's total land and water area is 77,116 square miles (199,730 sq km). It is the 17th-largest state. The state capital is Pierre.

East of the Missouri River, the land has been shaped by Ice Age glaciers. The terrain is mostly flat, with some rolling hills. The land in some places is dotted with small lakes, formed by the melting glaciers long ago.

The plains of South Dakota are ideal for farming. The soil is rich, and the flat land makes planting and harvesting easier. There are many farms that raise corn, soybeans, and wheat.

West of the Missouri River, the land is hillier, and more arid. It is part of the Great Plains. In places, there are steep ravines and buttes. There are also wide swaths of flat land suitable for growing wheat, hay, sunflowers, or for raising cattle.

Soybean Field

The Black Hills have many towering granite peaks, needles, cliffs, and spires.

In the southwest part of the state are the Badlands. They are home to steep cliffs, buttes, and ravines, with brightly colored layers of eroded rock. Early European settlers named them the Badlands because they were "a bad land to travel across."

In the far west-central part of South Dakota are the Black Hills. These low mountains got their name from the darkly colored evergreen trees that grow on their slopes. There are deep canyons, waterfalls, and towering rock formations. The state's highest point, Harney Peak, is in this region. It rises 7,242 feet (2,207 m).

Also in the Black Hills are two enormous rock sculptures carved into the granite mountains: Mount Rushmore National Memorial and nearby Crazy Horse Memorial. While they are major American icons, they are also controversial. Many Native Americans consider the Black Hills to be sacred ground that has been marred by the giant sculptures.

GEOGRAPHY

CLIMATE AND
WEATHER

South Dakota has a continental climate, with four distinct seasons. Temperatures can often be extreme, with roasting-hot summers and bone-chilling winters. There are also many pleasant days. The average July high temperature is 86°F (30°C). The record high temperature occurred in Usta on July 15, 2006. On that day, the thermometer soared to 120°F (49°C). In contrast, the record low temperature is a teeth-chattering -58°F (-50°C). It occurred in the town of McIntosh on February 17, 1936.

*A rainbow forms after a summer
rain in Custer State Park.*

An 1880s-era train chugs through a snowstorm as it carries tourists between Hill City and Keystone, South Dakota. In parts of the Black Hills, snowfall can reach 100 inches (254 cm) or more each winter.

Statewide, South Dakota receives 20 inches (51 cm) of precipitation yearly. More rain falls in the eastern part of the state than in the arid west. The west also receives less snow. However, in parts of the Black Hills, snowfall can often reach 100 inches (254 cm) or more.

Extreme weather sometimes strikes South Dakota. It includes droughts, blizzards, thunderstorms, lightning, and large hail. The eastern part of the state is in Tornado Alley, where deadly twisters are more common than in other parts of the country.

CLIMATE AND WEATHER

PLANTS AND
ANIMALS

Before European settlers came to South Dakota in the mid-1800s, most of the land was covered with tall prairie grasses. Early pioneers wrote that the land was like an ocean of grass.

Today, much of South Dakota's prairies have been plowed over and converted to farmland. However, there is still much prairie land remaining. Plants found on the prairies include big bluestem, little bluestem, western wheatgrass, blue grama, switchgrass, Indiangrass, goldenrod, coneflower, and prairie clover. In the more arid western part of the state are blue grama, buffalo grass, and prickly pear cactus.

A western diamondback rattlesnake next to a prickly pear cactus in South Dakota.

Much of South Dakota's prairie landscape is treeless. Only three percent of the state is forested. However, along riverbeds and lakeshores, trees such as cottonwoods, willows, and elms can be found. There are millions of ponderosa pine trees growing in the heavily forested mountains of the Black Hills, in western South Dakota. The Black Hills spruce is the official state tree. Other trees found growing in the Black Hills include lodgepole pine, aspen, bur oak, and birch.

Many types of trees grow along the banks of a stream in the Black Hills.

Prairie Dogs

Many kinds of wildflowers bloom on the prairies and in the mountain woodlands of South Dakota. They include black-eyed Susans, goldenrod, poppies, bluebells, and larkspurs. The pasque is the official state flower. The beautiful purple flower is most often found on hillsides or in wooded pine forests.

Dozens of animal species make their home on South Dakota's prairies. They include mule deer, pronghorn, prairie dogs, shrews, bats, kangaroo rats, spotted skunks, jackrabbits, and coyotes. The coyote is the official state animal. White-tailed deer are found throughout South Dakota.

The Black Hills are home to many species of animals. Commonly spotted are pronghorn, bison, elk, beavers, bobcats, bighorn sheep, mountain goats, and porcupines.

Pronghorns rest on South Dakota prairie grass.

More than 300 species of birds can be found in South Dakota's blue skies. Bald eagles and golden eagles can often be spotted along the Missouri River, along with many kinds of ducks and geese. Living on the plains are grouse and prairie chickens. Wild turkeys roost in the Black Hills. The official state bird of South Dakota is the ring-necked pheasant. Other common birds include osprey, owls, gulls, terns, chickadees, finches, pelicans, egrets, woodpeckers, American robins, and jays.

Fish that swim in South Dakota's lakes, rivers, and streams include carp, suckers, bullheads, catfish, northern pike, muskellunge, rainbow trout, brook trout, white bass, sunfish, bluegill, crappies, walleye, and smallmouth and largemouth bass. Fish found mainly in the waters of the Missouri River include sturgeon, gar, paddlefish, Chinook salmon, and brown trout.

South Dakota's official state insect is the honeybee. They are valued by farmers, who count on the hard-working insects to pollinate plants.

Grouse

Prairie Chicken

HISTORY

The first people to live in present-day South Dakota came to the area about 10,000 years ago, perhaps much earlier. These Paleo-Indians were the ancient ancestors of today's Native Americans. They were nomads who hunted herds of large animals such as bison and mastodons. They eventually settled into villages. Some of them built large earthen mounds for religious ceremonies such as burials.

By the time the first European explorers came to South Dakota in the late 1600s and 1700s, several major Native American tribes had formed. They included the Arikara, Cheyenne, and Sioux tribes.

A Native American hunts a bison on foot on the Great Plains.

A Sioux council painted by George Catlin in 1847. The Sioux lived in bison-hide tents called teepees.

The Arikara people lived peacefully and farmed mainly along the Missouri River. They hunted bison and built earthen lodges. The Sioux (also called the Lakota) lived mainly on the plains. They sometimes fought rival groups for territory and to control trade. The Sioux lived in bison-hide tents called teepees.

In 1743, the first Europeans arrived in the South Dakota area. They were two brothers, Francois and Louis-Joseph La Vérendrye. They were French fur traders. They buried a lead tablet near the present-day capital of Pierre, South Dakota. Writing on the tablet claimed the area for France.

In 1803, the United States paid France $15 million for a huge piece of land called the Louisiana Purchase. (Today's state of Louisiana was just a small part of the area.) The sale almost doubled the size of the United States. Present-day South Dakota was part of the purchase.

President Thomas Jefferson chose Meriwether Lewis and William Clark to lead an expedition, called the Corps of Discovery, to explore the new land. In 1804, the expedition started at the mouth of the Missouri River. They reached present-day South Dakota in August, then continued upriver. After traveling to the Pacific Ocean, they came through the South Dakota area again on their return journey in 1806.

Lewis and Clark Expedition reenactors land their keelboat at the confluence of the Missouri and Bad Rivers, near Pierre, South Dakota. The site is where the Corps of Discovery narrowly avoided a skirmish with the Teton Sioux in 1804.

Artist Karl Bodmer painted Fort Pierre and the Missouri River in 1833.

In 1817, American fur traders built a permanent post near the present-day city of Pierre. Over the next several decades, fur traders, farmers, and ranchers began settling the land. In the 1850s, the United States Army built Fort Randall along the Missouri River. More settlers poured into the area.

By the 1830s, many Native Americans had died or been forced off their land. Diseases such as smallpox and measles wiped out entire villages. The Native Americans had no natural immunity to the deadly infections.

On March 2, 1861, the United States government organized Dakota Territory. It included the present-day states of South Dakota, North Dakota, Montana, and parts of Wyoming and Nebraska.

As more people came to Dakota Territory, several Native American tribes, especially the Sioux, were faced with the loss of their traditional hunting grounds. They fought back against the white settlers.

Lieutenant Colonel George Custer lead an 1874 expedition across the plains of Dakota Territory.

In 1868, the United States gave ownership of the Black Hills to the Sioux. In 1874, gold was discovered in the area by an expedition led by Lieutenant Colonel George Custer. Miners and settlers illegally flooded into the Black Hills.

From 1876 to 1877, the Great Sioux War raged across the plains. Sioux and Cheyenne Native Americans battled the United States Army. The Army eventually won, and the Native Americans were forced once again to give away their land and move to reservations.

In the 1880s, railroads were built across the South Dakota prairies. Many immigrants arrived from Germany, Scandinavia, Ireland, and Russia. They faced harsh winters, spring floods, and hot summers. However, many were successful. Large farms grew fields of profitable wheat. Many cattle were raised on the open plains. New towns sprang up along the railroad tracks.

Lawmakers split Dakota Territory. On November 2, 1889, both South and North Dakota were admitted to the United States. South Dakota became the 40th state.

Soil drifts over a South Dakota hog house in 1935.

The Great Depression of the 1930s hit South Dakota hard. Many people lost their jobs, farms, and homes. In addition to the bad economy, a long drought caused crops to wither in the fields. Enormous dust storms blew away fertile topsoil, and swarms of grasshoppers ate whatever was left. The region became known as the Dust Bowl.

During World War II (1939-1945), the economy improved and the rains returned. South Dakota's crops and cattle were in high demand by a hungry nation. Large dams were constructed on the Missouri River to control flooding and create electricity. In the 2000s, South Dakota has come to rely less on agriculture and more on service industries such as finance and tourism.

South Dakota's cattle help feed a hungry nation.

DID YOU KNOW?

• In 1890, more than 250 Sioux Native American men, women, and children were killed in a battle that came to be known as the Wounded Knee Massacre. In December 1890, large numbers of Sioux gathered on the Pine Ridge Reservation to perform a religious ceremony called the Ghost Dance. It symbolized the eventual return of their ancestors and their hunting grounds. The United States Army was worried the Ghost Dance ceremonies would cause violence. Soldiers from the 7th Cavalry were sent to the reservation to disarm the Native Americans. A group of Sioux surrendered near Wounded Knee Creek. Tensions were high. A shot rang out. The soldiers believed they were under attack and began shooting. The Sioux started shooting back. By the time the smoke cleared, hundreds of Sioux were dead. At least 25 soldiers were also killed.

Benjamin Harrison

• On November 2, 1889, President Benjamin Harrison signed two laws that divided Dakota Territory in half and created both North and South Dakota. But which state came first? Nobody knows for sure because President Harrison kept it a secret. He shuffled the admission papers of the two Dakotas and blindly signed them. Only later was it decided that North Dakota was admitted first, as the 39th state, while South Dakota became the 40th state. The order was probably determined alphabetically.

• In the late 1870s, lawless mining towns such as Deadwood sprang up in the Black Hills. Fortune seekers came from all over the country,

The Homestake Mine

including colorful Western characters such as Wild Bill Hickok, Calamity Jane, and Seth Bullock. The most successful mine was in nearby Lead. The Homestake Mine eventually produced more than 41 million ounces (1.2 billion g) of gold and 9 million ounces (255 million g) of silver. Today, the deep mine shafts are used for scientific research.

DID YOU KNOW?

PEOPLE

Laura Ingalls Wilder (1867-1957) wrote the beloved *Little House on the Prairie* series of children's books. Although born in Wisconsin, she moved with her family to De Smet, Dakota Territory (in today's eastern South Dakota) in 1879, when she was just 12. Wilder spent the rest of her childhood in the De Smet area. She and her pioneer family endured

many hardships, including drought, fire, and sickness, while struggling to make a living on the wild frontier. Later in life, she wrote novels that were inspired by her real-life experiences. For example, she and her family endured one of the harshest winters ever recorded in 1880-1881. It played a big part in her book *The Long Winter*, in which the fictional snowbound pioneer family nearly starves to death. Wilder wrote a total of nine *Little House* books.

Seth Bullock

(1849-1919) was a larger-than-life Western lawman who spent most of his life in the gold-rush town of Deadwood, South Dakota. He was born in present-day Ontario, Canada. As a teenager, he moved to Helena, Montana Territory, to escape his abusive father. He became a lawmaker and a sheriff. In 1876, he and his

friend, Sol Star, moved to lawless Deadwood, Dakota Territory. They opened a hardware store, selling goods to gold miners. One day after they arrived, Western legend Wild Bill Hickok was murdered playing poker in a local saloon. People demanded better protection. Bullock became Deadwood's first sheriff. He and his deputies quickly established law and order. Bullock later became a United States Marshal for South Dakota. Today, Seth Bullock is buried in Mount Moriah Cemetery on a hillside overlooking Deadwood.

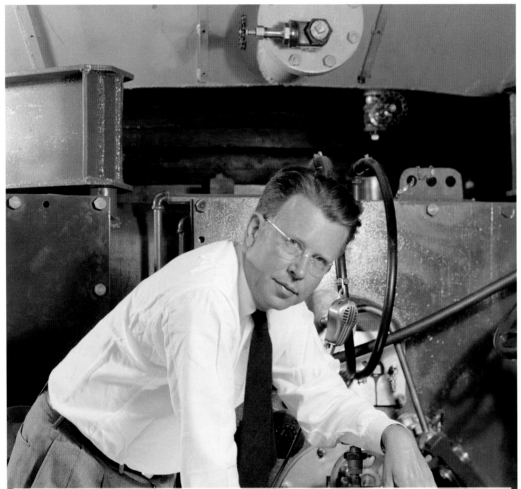

Ernest Orlando Lawrence (1901-1958) was a scientist best known for inventing the cyclotron. Often nicknamed an "atom smasher," a cyclotron sends atoms through giant, circular tubes. The atoms then crash into each other, and the reactions are analyzed. Lawrence was born in Canton, South Dakota. He attended college at the University of South Dakota in the city of Vermillion. For his work on the cyclotron, he was awarded the Nobel Prize in Physics in 1939. During World War II, in the early 1940s, Lawrence helped the United States develop the first atomic bombs. An atomic element (lawrencium) is named in his honor.

Sitting Bull (1831-1890) was a member of the Lakota Sioux. He was born in Dakota Territory. In his youth, Sitting Bull was a skilled and brave warrior who fought in many battles. He became a holy man who guided his people. He resisted attempts by the United States government to force Native Americans to live on reservations. In 1876, he rallied his people to victory over the U.S. 7th Cavalry at the Battle of the Little Bighorn in Montana. After the battle, Sitting Bull fled with a group of Lakota to Canada. In 1881, he returned to the United States and surrendered. In 1890, he was shot and killed during a struggle with police on the Standing Rock Indian Reservation in South Dakota.

CITIES

Sioux Falls is the largest city in South Dakota. Its population is about 171,544. It is located in the southeastern part of the state, near the falls of the Big Sioux River. It began in the 1860s as a center for farming, meatpacking, and stone quarrying. Today, the city's factories also produce farm and construction equipment, plastics, and electronics. Service industries such as banking and health care are also important. Washington Pavilion, in downtown Sioux Falls, is a center for art and entertainment. It is the home of the South Dakota Symphony Orchestra, art galleries, a dome theater, and the Kirby Science Discovery Center. The Great Plains Zoo & Delbridge Museum of Natural History is a 45-acre (18-ha) park that features more than 1,000 animals from all over the world.

Pierre (pronounced "peer") is the capital of South Dakota. Its population is about 14,002. It is located near the center of the state, along the east bank of the Missouri River. It is the second-least populated state capital in the country (after Montpelier, Vermont). In the early 1800s, a fur-trading post called Fort Pierre was located on the other side of the river. In 1880, a railroad was built that stopped at the east bank. The settlement that sprang up along the tracks became Pierre. The town was founded that year. Pierre became a regional trading center for cattle and other goods. It was named the state capital in 1889. Today, Pierre remains an important agricultural center. Vacationers also enjoy fishing and boating on the Missouri River. The impressive state capitol building is made of sandstone, limestone, and Italian marble.

Rapid City is the second-largest city in South Dakota. Its population is about 73,569. It is located on the east side of the Black Hills. It was founded in 1876 by miners who had been looking for gold in the mountains. It became a railroad hub starting in the 1880s, and grew as a center for trade. Nearby military air and missile bases built in the mid-1900s helped the city grow. Today, Rapid City has a strong economy based on manufacturing, government services, health care, and tourism. The South Dakota School of Mines and Technology houses the Museum of Geology, which features minerals and dinosaur bones found in the Black Hills and nearby Badlands. Another popular Rapid City attraction is Dinosaur Park. Built in 1936, it features five life-sized concrete sculptures of prehistoric beasts on a hill overlooking the city.

Dinosaur Park

Aberdeen is located in the northeastern corner of South Dakota. It is the state's third-largest city. Its population is about 28,102. It was founded in 1881 when a railroad was built through the area. Aberdeen was named after the city of Aberdeen, Scotland, the hometown of the railroad's president. Today, Aberdeen is a center for agriculture, health care, retail, and education. The city is home to Northern State University, which enrolls more than 2,500 students annually.

Wild Bill's Grave

Deadwood is a historic town in the Black Hills. Its population is about 1,258. In 1876, gold was discovered in the area. Deadwood served thousands of miners and others who came seeking their fortunes. Today, there are resorts, casinos, museums, and shops for the many tourists who visit each year. Buried in Mount Moriah Cemetery are Western legends Wild Bill Hickok, Calamity Jane, and Seth Bullock.

TRANSPORTATION

Throughout the late 1800s, railroads helped South Dakota grow. Towns sprang up along the tracks, and the state's crops could be moved quickly to faraway markets. Today, 9 freight railroads operate in the state on 1,753 miles (2,821 km) of track. The most common goods hauled by trains include farm and food products, coal, chemicals, and cement.

There are 82,558 miles (132,864 km) of public roadways in South Dakota. Interstate I-90 travels east and west across the lower third of the state. It connects the cities of Sioux Falls, Mitchell, Rapid City, and Spearfish. Interstate I-29 runs north and south on the far eastern side of the state. It also passes through Sioux Falls.

There are more than 175 airports in South Dakota. Most are small. Major commercial airports serve the cities of Sioux Falls, Aberdeen, Pierre, Rapid City, Watertown, and Huron. The busiest airport is Sioux Falls Regional Airport. It serves nearly one million passengers yearly.

Grain silos stand next to a freight train in Wall, South Dakota. Trains are essential for transporting farm products.

NATURAL RESOURCES

Agriculture is a big part of South Dakota's economy. In the western part of the state, there are huge open areas where cattle can graze. The state makes almost as much money raising beef cattle, hogs, sheep, and poultry as it does raising crops.

There are about 31,300 farms in South Dakota. Many are very large. Their average size is 1,383 acres (560 ha). The most valuable crops raised include corn, soybeans, hay, wheat, sunflowers, sorghum, oats, beans, flaxseed, and barley. Most of South Dakota's corn is used to feed cattle or to produce ethanol fuel.

Four combines are used in tandem to harvest a South Dakota wheat field.

In the Black Hills, there are several mines where gold and precious gems are dug from the Earth. The Homestake Mine, near the town of Lead, was one of the most productive gold mines in the world. It ceased production in 2001, but there are other places where gold continues to be mined. Other products mined in South Dakota include gypsum, silver, copper, plus sand and gravel.

South Dakota is a major producer of hydroelectricity, most of which it sells to neighboring states. Large dams on the Missouri River in South Dakota include the Fort Randall, Garrison, Oahe, and Gavins Point Dams.

Torrents of water from the Missouri River roar through the Gavins Point Dam just outside of Yankton, South Dakota. Gavins Point is one of several South Dakota dams that are used to generate hydroelectricity.

NATURAL RESOURCES

INDUSTRY

South Dakota's factories produce many kinds of goods. They include food products, machinery, finished wood products, plastics, and electronics.

In recent decades, the service industry has become a much larger part of South Dakota's economy. Instead of making products, companies in the service industry sell services to other businesses and consumers. The industry includes businesses such as advertising, banking, financial services, health care, insurance, restaurants, retail stores, law, marketing, and tourism. About 60 percent of South Dakotans are employed in the service industry.

Reptile Gardens is a popular wild animal park near Rapid City, South Dakota. Opened in 1937, the park draws thousands of tourists each year.

A B-1B Lancer takes off from Ellsworth Air Force Base near Rapid City, South Dakota. This base, and other U.S. government agencies in South Dakota, are important employers for the state.

Many financial companies, such as Citibank, have large operations in South Dakota, thanks to favorable state laws and regulations. South Dakota also benefits from government employers such as Ellsworth Air Force Base near Rapid City.

Tourism is a huge part of South Dakota's economy. Approximately 14 million people vacation in the state each year to visit Mount Rushmore, Deadwood, and the Black Hills, as well as go camping, hunting, and fishing. Visitors spend nearly $4 billion each year, which supports jobs for more than 52,000 South Dakotans.

SPORTS

There are no professional major league sports teams in South Dakota. However, Sioux Falls and Rapid City have several minor league and independent league teams. The Sioux Falls Skyforce is a National Basketball Association (NBA) development team affiliated with the Miami Heat. Other minor league sports represented in South Dakota include ice hockey, arena football, and baseball.

South Dakota has two universities that compete in National Collegiate Athletic Association (NCAA) Division I sporting events. South Dakota State University, in Brookings, is the home of the Jackrabbits. Sports teams from the University of South Dakota, in Vermillion, are called the Coyotes (pronounced "ki yotes").

Jack the Jackrabbit is the mascot for South Dakota State University, Brookings.

Charlie the Coyote is the mascot for the University of South Dakota, Vermillion.

A hiker stands at the top of Harney Peak Trail overlooking the Black Hills.

South Dakota has much to offer outdoor sports lovers. People enjoy fishing, hunting, camping, and rock climbing. There are hundreds of miles of hiking and bicycling trails in places like Black Hills National Forest, Custer State Park, Badlands National Park, and many others. One of the most popular hikes is the Harney Peak Trail. There are spectacular views of the Black Hills at the summit. It is the highest spot in South Dakota, rising 7,242 feet (2,207 m) above sea level.

ENTERTAINMENT

More than three million people visit Mount Rushmore National Memorial each year to gaze at the 60-foot (18-m) -high faces of Presidents George Washington, Thomas Jefferson, Theodore Roosevelt, and Abraham Lincoln. Just a short drive away is the Crazy Horse Memorial. Sculptor Korczak Ziolkowski started work on the carved granite tribute to the famous Native American leader in 1948. When finished, the massive statue will be 641 feet (195 m) long and 563 feet (172 m) high.

South Dakota is home to two spectacular national parks. Badlands National Park is a maze of eroded, multi-hued buttes, spires, and canyons. The park is also filled with easy-to-spot wildlife such as prairie dogs and pronghorn. Wind Cave National Park takes visitors deep underground to one of the longest cave systems in the world. On the surface, bison and elk are often seen.

A small plaster sculpture of the Crazy Horse Memorial stands at the visitor center below the mountain. The massive statue has been in progress since 1948.

The world's only Corn Palace is in the town of Mitchell. Each year, the exterior of the building is decorated with giant murals made from corn and other grains. The multipurpose arena hosts concerts, sporting events, and more.

No vacation to South Dakota is complete without a visit to Wall Drug. The collection of drug stores, gifts shops, and amusements is located in the town of Wall, just north of Badlands National Park. There's always free ice water for thirsty travelers. You can even sit on a giant jackalope!

Visitors to Wall, South Dakota, stop at Wall Drug to enjoy free ice water and family fun.

ENTERTAINMENT

TIMELINE

8,000 BC— The first Paleo-Indians arrive in present-day South Dakota.

1700s—Arikara, Cheyenne, and Sioux Native Americans settle in the South Dakota area.

1743—The first European explorers visit the area. Francois and Louis-Joseph La Vérendrye claim the area for France.

1800s—The Sioux become the most powerful tribe in South Dakota.

1803—France sells the Louisiana Purchase to the United States. Present-day South Dakota is included in this large land transfer.

1804—Lewis and Clark explore South Dakota along the Missouri River.

1817—The first fur-trading post, near the present-day city of Pierre, is established.

1861—Dakota Territory is organized by the United States government.

1873—Railroads are built through to Yankton.

1874—Gold is discovered in the Black Hills.

1889—South Dakota becomes the 40th state in the Union.

1929—The beginning of the Great Depression and the Dust Bowl era.

1941-1945—American involvement in World War II. The economy of South Dakota begins to grow again.

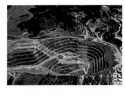

2001—The Homestake Mine in Lead ceases production. At the time, it was the oldest, deepest, and largest gold mine in America.

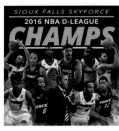

2016—The Sioux Falls Skyforce basketball team wins the NBA D-League championship.

GLOSSARY

BADLANDS

An area deeply eroded by wind and water, with high cliffs, low valleys, and many buttes.

BLACK HILLS

A mountainous, wooded area in western South Dakota.

BUTTE

A tall, steep hill with a flat top. Similar to a mesa, but smaller.

DUST BOWL

In the 1930s, the Great Plains region of the United States, including the state of South Dakota, was over-farmed and then had little rain for several years. High winds swept across the dry land, creating huge dust storms.

ETHANOL

A fuel made partially from corn. It is used as an alternative to gasoline in automobiles.

GLACIERS

Huge, slow-moving sheets of ice that grow and shrink as the climate changes. During the Ice Age, some glaciers covered entire regions and measured more than one mile (1.6 km) thick.

GREAT DEPRESSION

A time of worldwide economic hardship beginning in 1929. Many people lost their jobs and had little money. The Great Depression finally eased in the mid-1930s, but didn't end until many countries entered World War II, around 1939.

GREAT PLAINS

The land east of the Rocky Mountains, west of the Mississippi River and stretching from Canada to the Mexican border. It is mostly covered with grass and few trees.

JACKALOPE

A mythical beast that resembles a jackrabbit with antelope horns.

LOUISIANA PURCHASE

A purchase by the United States from France in 1803 of a huge section of land west of the Mississippi River. The United States nearly doubled in size after the purchase. The young country paid $15 million for approximately 828,000 square miles (2.1 million sq km) of land.

NOBEL PRIZE

An award given each year to someone who has made important achievements in a particular area of study. There are six awards: chemistry, physics, physiology/medicine, literature, economics, and peace.

SIOUX

A Native American tribe that lived in South Dakota by the time Europeans arrived. The Sioux fought many battles to try to save their lands.

TORNADO ALLEY

An area of the United States that has many tornadoes. There is no official boundary for Tornado Alley. Many maps show that it stretches from Texas in the south to North Dakota in the north. Some sources say it reaches east all the way to western Ohio.

WORLD WAR II

A conflict that was fought from 1939 to 1945, involving countries around the world. The United States entered the war after Japan bombed the American naval base at Pearl Harbor, in Oahu, Hawaii, on December 7, 1941.

INDEX